How Aging
Affects
Belt Height

Other Books by Dan Reynolds

Now They All Have Window Seats!

Christmas Meltdown

Birthday Bash!

How Aging Affects Affects Belt Height

A Reynolds Unwrapped Cartoon Colletion

Dan Reynolds

Andrews McMeel
Publishing

Kansas City

How Aging Affects Belt Height

07 08 WKT 10 9 8 7 6 5

ISBN: 0-7407-4714-2

Library of Congress Control Number: 2004101567

www.reynoldsunwrapped.com

ATTENTION: SCHOOLS AND BUSINESSES

Andrews McMeel books are available at quantity discounts with bulk purchase for educational, business, or sales promotional use. For information, please write to: Special Sales Department, Andrews McMeel Publishing, LLC, 4520 Main Street, Kansas City, Missouri 64111.

Foreword

During my search to find the perfect person to write a foreword for my collection of cartoons on aging, I stumbled upon an article in my local newspaper. The article was about the oldest man in America, Fred Hale Sr., a 112-year-old who lived in Baldwinsville, New York. He also happens to  be, at this writing, the oldest man in the world. Fred is in the *Guinness Book of World Records* as the oldest licensed driver in America, a feat he accomplished while still driving at 107 years old. He was also the state of Maine's oldest beekeeper. He kept bees from age 17 to age 107. I thought that was interesting, since he was now residing in a town known as "B-ville."

To give you a sense of how old Fred is, consider the following: When Fred was born on December 1, 1890, there were only forty-four stars in the United States flag. Benjamin Harrison was the U.S. president. We were still fighting the Native Americans at Wounded Knee. Forget about television or movies; radio hadn't even been invented! The year Fred was born was the same year Vincent Van Gogh died. Fred was already eight years old when the Spanish-American War broke out. He was born before Rudolf Diesel invented the diesel-fueled internal combustion engine. Before Fred was born, there was no such thing as a zipper, or America's first gasoline-powered automobile.

With the help of his youngest son, Fred Hale Jr. (who's no spring chicken himself at eighty-two years young), I was able to get Fred Sr. to graciously agree to foreword this book.

Turns out Fred was unable to write the foreword, but I asked him a series of questions and his responses are below:

Dan: How are you, Mr. Hale?

Fred: [Shakes his head "no."]

Dan: Can I call you Fred? [Fred's son tells me I can.]

Dan: What's your secret to a long life, Fred?

Fred: No secret. Haven't any . . . maybe bee pollen and honey.

Dan: How long were you married?

Fred: I don't remember . . . sixty-eight years? I never used a pencil. Whatever I couldn't remember [without the use of a pencil] was gone. [Long pause.] And I couldn't remember much.

Dan: Times change. Do you think people have changed over the last hundred years?

Fred: People are the same.

Dan: What is your fondest memory?

Fred: I don't know.

Dan: What's the most important lesson life has taught you?

Fred: Keep busy and keep out of mischief.

Dan: Did humor play a part of living a long time?

Fred: No.

Dan: What did?

Fred: Work.

Dan: How would you like to be remembered?

Fred: [My] work. When I had time off, I still worked.

Dan: Do you remember being a kid?

Fred: A little.

Dan: Have you ever met anyone famous?

Fred: Ted Williams two or three times.

Dan: Did you ever read cartoons?

Fred: Cartoons in *Reader's Digest*.

Dan: That's interesting. I happen to be a cartoonist who has had many cartoons in that magazine.

Fred: [No response.]

Dan: One more question, Fred. When you get to heaven, what do you think God will say to you?

Fred: What took you so long?

~

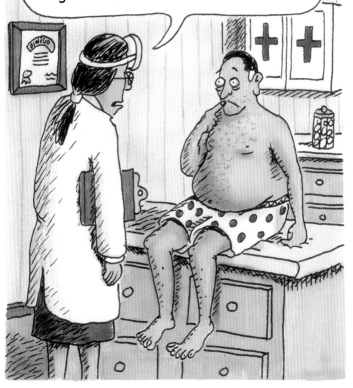

"Mortimer, quit referring to the **bags** under my eyes. You're really starting to freak me out."

Somehow Cheryl ends up with thinner hair and more body.

"Straighten Up
and Fly Right"

"You might consider laying off the fast food for a while."

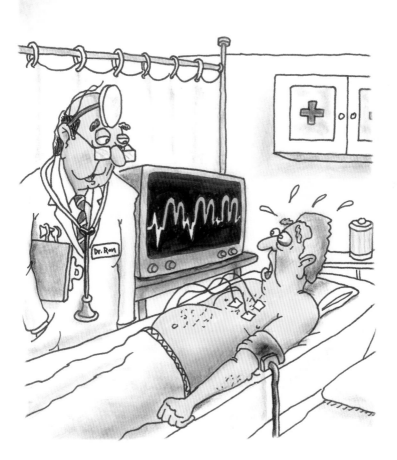

"Thank you for recognizing me.
Now, who exactly am I?"

The Denture Fairy

Peter, Paul, and Mary
the Early Years . . .

Jack and Jill Over the Hill

Disco Crossing

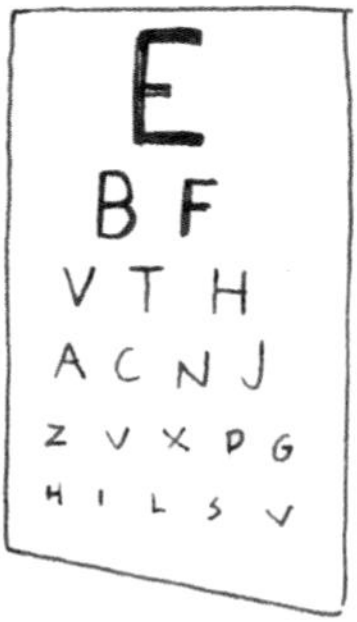
E
B F
V T H
A C N J
Z V X D G
H I L S V

Mary's wish to look like a million bucks comes true.

Elvis has leapt the building.

"Relax. I'm just your landscaper."

The Middle Ages

Weapons of Ass Reduction

After the kids grew up, the old lady sold the shoe and bought a summer home.

$ALE